Dating Struggles?

Don Barnes

Published by Don Barnes, 2024.

Table of Contents

When someone is struggling with a particular area or two, chances are they are "out of balance" with how life works. How does life work? Life works in threes. | If you're interested in personal topics like life, health, money or business topics like sales, time management and public speaking...TRYUNE WORKS! can shed some light on creating success

About the Author

Don is the founder and author of Life Works in Threes!™ E-books. He is a lifelong Texan who has traveled extensively while taking a keen interest in human behavior. His curiosity about life and what drives humans led him to the discovery of how life works in threes. He coined this term as the *Tryune Concept*.

Don attended college on an athletic scholarship and then embarked on a 30-year career in the oil and gas industry. Since the year 2000, he has been a consultant for distributors and manufacturers of various industries. Along the way, he worked on his Tryune discovery in hopes of someday sharing his findings with those struggling unnecessarily... in life. What Don surmised from 40+ years of R&D was that people were struggling unnecessarily because they were not aware that "life works in threes." They, for the most part, have been living their lives by chance rather than by choice, he also discovered.

From this, he began focusing on the "mechanics of life" which shows formulas for success with subjects such as *life, health, money, purpose and so forth*. When people are able to grasp the Tryune Concept, they can apply the formulas with topics that interest them and begin eliminating the struggle. This epiphany is what triggered his Tryune venture and is now on the path of sharing with all who desire to improve on their lives.

Don currently resides in Southern California and Texas while overseeing his businesses and investments.

Life Works in Threes™

When I was a kid growing up, no one sat me down and said, "Okay Don, I'm going to show you how life works so that you can navigate your way through adulthood." I graduated from school, got married and went about my way with the "learn as you go" concept. It was kind of like putting together a backyard swing set without a set of instructions. Lots of frustration and do-overs, for sure!

My discovery of the "triune" word and noticing how things come together in threes is really what set me off on researching that maybe "life comes in three" ...sort of a mechanical approach to managing life, if you will. I combed the libraries and bookstores for information on this and found one book on the subject that was written back in 1951. The author's name was John S. Arant.

What Mr. Arant had to say is this "For lack of a better name, I have called this *The Triangle of Triumph* and therefore, consistent with the name, since most of these conclusions are built on the geometric figure of the triangle." He continued "All Life and all lives are seated in, and circumscribed by, the triangle. The Author and Source and Director of all life is Himself triune in character – Father, Son, and Holy Spirit. Man is of triple nature – body, mind, and spirit – and within those three there are many triangles – desires, development, decay; intellect, will, sensibilities. Of this "paced interlude in the midst of eternity" which we call time there is the triangle of Past, Present, and Future. Space – that limitless and measureless element of the physical universe – is best known in terms of Height, Breadth, and Depth. Try building yourself some triangles along the lines of your Will, your Work, your Way – You will find some interesting angles.

So, for the first time, I realized that life is designed in a mechanical way to come in threes. That means you don't have to rely on wishing and hoping things turn out okay. You can actually look at the three parts that a particular thing is made of and then apply them to get what you're wanting. Like a three-ingredient recipe or a combination lock. With a combination lock, you need the three exact numbers to unlock the lock...otherwise you will continue to struggle.

Some 40 years later, I accumulated things that work in threes and that's when I knew I needed to share this with anyone wanting answers. To have success/harmony in your life, just apply the three parts of an area you're working on, and things will fall into place. I also learned that the recipe for success with just about anything is by doing these three things, consistently – THINK positively, SPEAK positively and ACT positively. For example, if I want to be a successful artist. I would think to myself "I can do this because I have the talent." Then I would speak it this way "Yes, I am working on my art degree and plan to do portraits professionally." Finally, I would act on that by taking art classes and continue crafting my skill. Eventually, I will see the positive results/success I'm looking for.

Conversely, if I think positively but speak negatively...it will cancel out. Or if I speak positively but have no positive action going on...nothing will happen.

I looked up "How Life Works" and "The Mechanics of Life" and these are really talking about the biology of how our cells work and other chemistry. TRYUNE WORKS! teaches that life is kind of like building blocks. Pick a topic you may be struggling with. See the three parts that topic consists of and then start applying them...on a consistent basis. That will help you overcome the struggle and get you back in harmony/success with how life works.

For 30+ years I was a golf instructor (by accident). My two kids had some success playing junior golf and so friends and neighbors would ask me to show them and their kids how to play golf successfully. From all of this, I got pretty good at watching golfers on the driving range and could spot right away why they were struggling with hitting bad golf shots. I was able to do that because I knew the three steps to hitting good golf shots. I learned them from studying golf and played for several decades. I "broke the code" for me so to speak.

So now you know that life works in threes. You can live your life *by choice* rather than *by chance* and that my friend... is the key to a fulfilling life.

LIFE WORKS
IN THREES!

My sanctuary on the Pacific coast

Introduction

Deciding to date people in today's world can feel like navigating a bustling marketplace where options abound, but finding the right fit takes a bit of savvy. It's a blend of old-school romance and modern pragmatism. In a sea of dating apps and social media profiles, the challenge isn't just meeting someone, but figuring out if they're genuinely compatible.

First off, there's the digital dilemma: swiping left or right can feel more like browsing through a catalog than finding a connection. It's tempting to judge potential partners by a handful of photos and a witty bio, but remember, real-life chemistry often surprises us. Putting yourself out there online is just the beginning; meaningful connections often blossom from genuine conversations and shared experiences beyond the screen.

Then there's the balancing act of expectations versus reality. In today's world, there's a wide spectrum of relationship styles and definitions. Whether you're looking for casual fun or a long-term commitment, being upfront about your intentions can save everyone involved a lot of confusion and heartache. Honesty and clear communication are key ingredients in any successful dating endeavor.

Ultimately, deciding to date in today's world means embracing the adventure with an open mind and heart. It's about discovering what you truly value in a partner and being willing to explore different avenues to find it. So, go ahead, swipe, chat, and meet up—just remember to stay true to yourself and enjoy the journey.

My discovery of the Tryune Concept

Before we dive into dating struggles and how to overcome them, let me share my discovery of the Tryune Concept and how life works in threes. It all began in the summer of 1982.

I grew up with parents who treated everyone with decency and respect. My three older sisters and I were raised in a home that was "middle-class traditional." We lived in modest homes in different small towns, attended school and church on a regular basis and celebrated all the traditional holidays. Eventually we settled during the spring of 1964 in the big city of Houston, Texas. I'll never forget the vastness of the city and hearing sirens from police cars, fire trucks and ambulances on a regular basis. I was excited and scared at the same time.

Once settled in this fast-paced city, I finished my growing-up years with an academic diploma and sweetheart intact. I got a job, bought a car, got married, bought a house and produced two beautiful babies in a span of about 5 years. Talk about having to grow up fast!

Things went from great in my childhood to absolute misery in my young adulthood. I began to struggle with my job because deep down I just hated what I was doing. This problem created a snowball effect because soon after, my weight, my finances, my relationships, my happiness and everything else worth saving was going down the drain. I eventually hit a level of frustration that I had never experienced before and didn't know how to get out of it. My cry for help was for anyone or anything to come to my rescue. I just ran out of solutions for my situation.

This is when my discovery happened.

One night shortly after my meltdown, while sleeping soundly, the word "triune" began to softly pound in my head like a mantra. I woke up a little startled and decided to go look up the word in my favorite dictionary (this was WAY before Google.) The definition said '**triune** (try-une) – 1) a group of three things; united. 2) Being 3 in 1 such as *humans are mental, physical and spiritual.* I scratched my head, got a glass of water and went back to bed.

The next day while driving around town, I began thinking about things that I was taught in my younger years that came in threes. My Boy Scout manual taught that to have **character**, I needed to be *1) physically strong,* 2) *mentally awake and 3) morally straight.* My high school football coach would say emphatically "If you want to be **a good football player**, you have to be *1) mobile 2) agile and 3) hostile!*" My first sales manager shared with me that to be **a successful salesman**, I needed to have *1) sales skills, 2) product knowledge and 3) a good image.*

"Hmm", I thought, "wonder if there are other examples out there of things that work in threes?" So, some 40 years later, I have researched and discovered that many, many things work in threes. What this message was telling me is that to achieve success or balance in any significant area of my life, the three things that area consisted of had to be present, continuously. That's when I had my epiphany. This discovery was telling me the secret to how life <u>really</u> works...in a mechanical way.

Tryune is a play on the word "triune" as an invitation to "try" this concept. Furthermore, we do not say that life <u>only</u> works in threes. Life also works in ones, twos, fours and so on. What has been observed though is that the many things significant to life, just so happen to come and work in threes. That's what is being shared in this book.

Now, you are about to see 40+ years of research and proof that life works in threes. I did not make up any of these topics. I invite you to research them on the internet to validate what is written here. There are some interesting facts that most of us have never realized...until now.

How Life Works in Threes (around 200 examples)

LIFE

Humans consist of *body, mind and soul.*

A human's basic needs are *health, income and provisions.*

A human's basic wants are *comfort, gain and approval.*

Our minds are made up of the *conscious, the subconscious and the unconscious.*

Philosophy explains *the id, the ego and superego.*

Atoms consist of *protons, neutrons and electrons.*

Motion is explained by *three basic laws.*

Science falls under three main branches: *natural, social and formal sciences*

Time is *past, present and future*...at the same time.

Electricity consists of *ohms, amperes and voltage.*

Music's basic elements are *duration, pitch and timbre.*

Democracy is a government *of the people, by the people and for the people.*

U.S. branches of government are *the judicial, the executive and the legislative.*

Armed Forces protect us on *land, air and sea.*

Environmentally, we are asked *to reduce, recycle and re-use.*

The news program gives us *the news, sports and conditions.*

Our days consist of *morning, afternoon and evening.*

Three months in each season of the year

Our main meals are known as *breakfast, lunch and dinner.*

A balanced diet consists of *good proteins, carbohydrates and fats.*

Traditional Family consists of *father, mother, and child(ren)*

SCIENCES

Three major branches of natural science – *(physical, earth/ space and life sciences)*

Three major branches of modern physics - *(classical, relativistic, quantum)*

Three major branches of biology *(botany, zoology, microbiology)*

Three spatial dimensions: *height* (up/down), *width* (left/ right) and *depth* (forwards/backwards)

Three-gauge bosons (photon, gluon, W&Z bosons)

Three types of elementary particles *(leptons, quarks, gauge bosons)*

Three quarks in every proton *(two "up" and one "down")*

Three primary colors of light *(red, green, blue)*

Three color tone properties *(hue, value, chroma)*

Three laws of motion *(Newton's laws)*

Three laws of planetary motion *(Kepler's laws)*

Three layers of the Sun's interior *(core, radiative zone, convective zone)*

Three layers of the Sun's atmosphere *(photosphere, chromosphere, corona)*

Three types of meteorites *(iron, stony iron, stony)*

Three types of galaxy shapes *(elliptical, spiral, irregular)*

Three substances of the universe *(normal matter, 'dark matter', 'dark energy')*

Three phases of the moon *(new moon, first quarter, full moon)*

Three planetary regions *(temperate, sub-tropical, tropical)*

Three layers of the Earth *(crust, mantle, core)*

Three components of an ecosystem *(producers, consumers, decomposers)*

Three types of rocks *(igneous, sedimentary, metamorphic)*

Three types of fossil fuels *(coal, crude oil, natural gas)*

Three hydrological processes *(evaporation, condensation, precipitation)*

Three basic types of (meteorological) precipitation *(liquid, freezing, frozen)*

Three types of substances *(mono-constituent, multi-constituent, UVCB)*

Three phases of (normal) matter *(solid, liquid, gas)*

Three types of covalent chemical bonds *(single, double and triple bonds)*

Three isotopes of hydrogen *(protium, deuterium, tritium)*

Three atoms in each molecule of water (*two hydrogen atoms and an oxygen atom*)

Three endings to salts (*-ide, -ite, -ate*)

Three requirements for fire (*fuel, oxygen, heat*)

Three nucleotide bases in a genetic codon

Three domains of life (*archaea, bacteria and eukaryotes*)

Three major groups of flowering plants (*monocots, eudicots, magnolids*)

Three major functions that are basic to plant growth and development: (*photosynthesis* [making sugars], *respiration* [metabolizing those sugars], and *transpiration* [water vapor loss]

Three things that the chlorophyll in plants needs for photosynthesis to take place: (*sunlight, carbon dioxide and water*)

Transpiration serves three roles: (*cooling the plant, moving minerals* and *sugars through the plant,* and *maintaining the turgidity pressure* [stiffness] *of the plant's cells*)

Three parts of an insect's body (*head, thorax, abdomen*)

BIOLOGY

Three types of cones in the retina, relating to the three primary colors

Three semi-circular canals in the ear *(lateral, anterior, posterior)*

Three sections in the ear *(outer, middle, inner)*

Three ossicles in the middle ear *(malleus, incus, stapes)*

Three segments to each limb *(proximal, mid, distal)*

Three bones in each arm *(humerus, radius, ulna)*

Three joints in the arm *(shoulder, elbow, wrist)*

Three joints in the leg *(hip, knee, ankle)*

Three joints in the elbow *(humeroulnar, humeroradial, proximal radioulnar)*

Three functional compartments in the knee joint *(the femoropatellar, medial femorotibial* and *lateral femorotibial articulations)*

Three types of fibrous joints *(sutures, gomphoses, syndesmoses)*

Three types of bone in each hand *(carpals, metacarpals, phalanges)*

Three types of bone in each foot (*tarsals, metatarsals, phalanges*)

Three bones (phalanges) in each finger and in each toe (*proximal, intermediate, distal*)

Three layers of skin (*dermis, epidermis, hypodermis*)

Three components of a cell (*cell membrane, nucleus, cytoplasm*)

Three types of blood vessels (*arteries, veins, capillaries*)

Three types of blood cells [*red* (erythrocytes), *white* (leukocytes), *platelets* (thrombocytes)]

Three processes of the intestinal tract (*ingestion, digestion, excretion*)

Three germ layers (*Endoderm, Mesoderm, Ectoderm*)

Three parts of a human tooth (*crown, neck, root*)

Three organs of otolaryngology (*ear, nose, throat*)

Three major body systems (*digestive, circulatory, respiratory*)

Three parts to a neuron: (*soma* [*cell body*], *axon, dendrites*)

Three main parts of the brain (*forebrain, midbrain, hindbrain*)

Three parts of the forebrain (*cerebrum, thalamus, hypothalamus*)

Three parts of the midbrain *(colliculi, tegmentum, cerebral peduncles)*

Three parts of the hindbrain *(cerebellum, pons, medulla)*

Three membranes enclosing the brain *(dura mater, arachnoid, pia mater)*

The brain operates on three levels: *consciously* (for cognitive thought and declarative memory); *subconsciously* (for pre-planned actions and procedural memory); and *unconsciously* (for breathing, heart beating, etc.)

Our conscious mind is fed from three sources: *our senses* (which can be fooled); *our memory* (which is flawed); and *our imagination* (which is inventive)

Three aspects of the human mind *(memory, intellect, will)*

Three parts of the human personality *(id, ego, superego)*

The sum of human capacity consists of three abilities *(thought, word and deed)*

Three times of man *(birth, life, death)*

Three periods of the Gait Cycle *(initial double limb support, single limb support, and terminal double limb support)*

MUSIC

Three types of musical notes *(sharps, flats, naturals)*

Three aspects of a song *(lyrics, melody, rhythm)*

Three types of musical chords *(root, third, fifth)*

MATHEMATICS

Three types of a real number (*positive, negative, zero*)

Three parts to any arithmetic operation: for addition: *augend, addend and sum* - for subtraction: *minuend, subtrahend and difference* - for multiplication: *multiplicand, multiplier and product* - for division: *dividend, divisor and quotient*

Three laws of arithmetic operations (*commutative, associative, distributive*)

Three types of equivalence relation (*reflexivity, symmetry, transitivity*)

Three types of symmetry operations (*translation, rotation, reflection*)

Three geometries (*Euclidean, spherical, hyperbolic*)

The number 3 is the basis of an entire branch of mathematics, called trigonometry (from the Greek *trigonon* "triangle" + *metron* "measure")

Three trigonometric functions (*sine, cosine, tangent*)

Three types of average (*mean, mode, median*)

GRAMMAR

Three logical operators (*AND, OR and NOT*)

Three laws of logic (*identity, noncontradiction, excluded middle*)

Three parts of a logical syllogism (*major premise, minor premise, conclusion*)

Three grammatical parts to a sentence (*subject, verb, complement*)

Three persons in grammar [*1st person* (I/we), *2nd* (you or your), *3rd* (he/she/it/they)]

Three genders in grammar [*masculine* (he/him), *feminine* (she/her), *neuter* (it)]

Three forms of comparison in grammar [*positive, comparative* (more, -er), *superlative* (most, -est)]

Three cases in (English) grammar [*subjective/nominative* (he), *objective/accusative* (him) and *possessive/genitive* (his)]

Three parts of a narrative (*beginning, middle, end*)

Components of an essay (*introduction, body, conclusion*)

Elements of a rhetorical appeal (*ethos, pathos, logos*)

Aspects of a story (*plot, characters, setting*)

RELIGION

The Creator – *omniscient, omnipotent, omnipresent*

Christian God – *Father, Son, Holy Spirit*

Jesus – *The Way, The Truth, The Life*

Ancient Near East- *Qudshu, Astarte, Anat*

Classical Antiquity – Many dieties came in threes

Hinduism – Para Brahman is *Brahma, Visnu, Shiva*

Ancient Celtic Cultures – *many example of triad dieties*

Buddhism – *The three jewels*

Taoism – *The three pure ones*

Islam – *Fear, Hope and Love*

Baha'i - *Intention, Power and Action*

Confucianism – *Benevolence, Wisdom and Courage*

OTHER TRIUNE EXAMPLES

3 Coins in a Fountain

3 Days of the Condor

3 Miles in a League

3 Goals in a Hat Trick

3 Piece Suit

3 Feet in a Yard

3 Books in Lord of the Rings

3 Ring Circus

3 Ships of Christopher Columbus

3 Sheets to the Wind

3 Books in a Trilogy

3 Wheels on a Tricycle

3 Wise Men

3-Legged Race

3 Ring Circus

3-Wheeler

3 Cornered Hat

3 Dimensional

3 Musketeers

3 R's (reading, 'riting, 'rithmatic)

3 Sides of a triangle

3 Races in the Triple Crown (horse racing)

3 Angles in a Triangle

3 Trimesters in a Pregnancy

3 Flavors in Neapolitan Ice Cream

3 Stars in Orion's belt

3 Barleycorns in an Inch

3 Hands on a Clock (with the Seconds Hand)

3 Colors in a Flag

3 Minute Egg

3 Great Pyramids at Giza

3 Holes in a Bowling Ball

3 Colors in a Set of Traffic Lights

3 Minutes in a Boxing Round

3 Teaspoons in a Tablespoon

3 Legs on a Stool

3 Monastic Vows (Obience, Stability, Conversatio Morum)

3 Body Types: Endomorph, Mesomorph, Ectomorph

3 Ring Notebooks

3 Germ layers: Endoderm, Mesoderm, Ectoderm

3 Species of Homo: Homo habilis, Homo erectus, Homo sapiens

3 Basic parts of a camera: Lens, Shutter, Sensor

3 Stages of a Project lifecycle: initiation, planning, execution

The Truth, The Whole Truth and Nothing but the Truth

Life, Liberty and the Pursuit of Happiness

Hear no Evil, See no Evil, Speak no Evil

National motto of France/Haiti: Liberty, Equality, Fraternity

Paper, Rock, Scissors

Ready, Aim, Fire

On Your mark, Get Set, Go

Olympic medals of gold, silver, bronze

Types of joints (ball & socket, hinge, pivot)

Stages of a rocket launch (launch, orbit, re-entry)

Parts of a joke (setup, delivery, punchline)

Primary components of a transistor (emitter, base, collector)

Primary components of an airplane (fuselage, wings, empennage)

Basic components of a computer: CPU, memory, storage

Three phases in the development of technology (*eotechnic* [*mechanical*], *paleotechnic* [*steam-powered*] and *neotechnic* [*electric-powered*]

Communication systems require three components (*transmitter, channel, receiver*)

The list goes on. See if you can find more examples as they are everywhere in our universe. Now that you know that life works in threes (with proof!), we can begin to apply this concept to whatever topics we want.

So, to overcome struggles with dating, we need to apply the three areas that dating consists of – LIST, PACKAGING and HEALTHY. Let's get started!

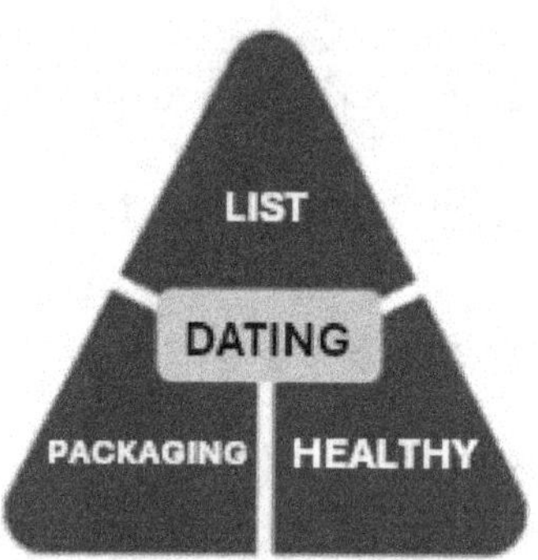
LIST
DATING
PACKAGING
HEALTHY

DATING

Making a list of what you find attractive in a potential partner can be a fun and insightful exercise! Think of it as crafting your personal wish list for a great companion. Whether it's a quirky sense of humor, shared interests like hiking or cooking, or qualities like kindness and ambition, jotting down these traits can help clarify what truly matters to you in a relationship. Remember, this list isn't set in stone—it's a starting point to understand your own preferences better and recognize them when you meet someone special. So, grab a pen and paper or create a digital note, and have fun brainstorming what makes your heart skip a beat!

Packaging yourself in a way that others find attractive is like presenting your best self to the world—it's not about changing who you are but highlighting your strengths and unique qualities. Just like choosing an outfit that makes you feel confident or polishing your resume for a job interview, how you present yourself matters in dating. This could mean taking care of your physical appearance, expressing your passions and interests with enthusiasm, or cultivating a positive attitude. Ultimately, it's about showing others the genuine, awesome person you are, so they can appreciate all the wonderful things you bring to the table. Finding that balance between authenticity and showcasing your best self can go a long way in making meaningful connections.

Searching for a healthy person to date is like choosing fresh ingredients for a delicious meal—you want something that nourishes and uplifts you. A healthy relationship starts with two individuals who are emotionally and mentally balanced, respecting each other's boundaries and supporting personal growth. It's about finding someone who communicates openly, handles conflicts constructively, and shares your values. When both partners are committed to their own well-being and the well-being of the relationship, it creates a foundation of trust and mutual respect. So, take your time to get to know someone beyond the surface level, observe how they handle challenges and treat others, and prioritize your own emotional health along the way. Healthy relationships are built on a solid foundation of understanding, kindness, and growth together.

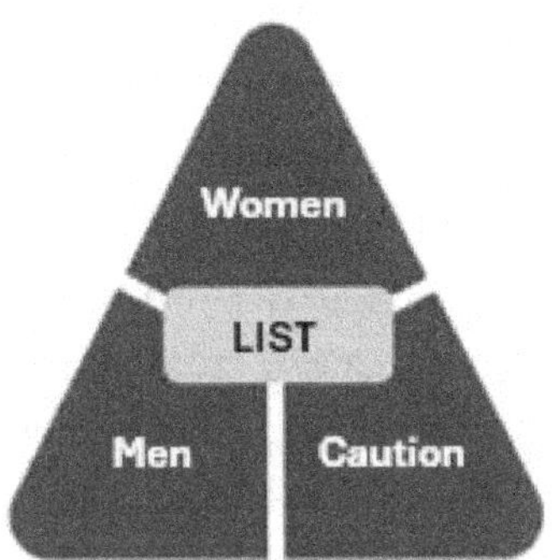

Women
LIST
Men
Caution

LIST

Making a list of what you're looking for in a mate can be a thoughtful and empowering exercise, guiding you towards the kind of relationship that truly resonates with your heart and values. Start by reflecting on qualities that are important to you—perhaps it's a shared sense of humor, ambition, or a passion for travel. These preferences can help clarify your desires and priorities, making it easier to recognize a good match when you meet them.

Next, consider the deeper aspects of compatibility beyond surface traits. Think about values, beliefs, and lifestyle preferences that align with your own. Are you seeking someone who values honesty and integrity as much as you do? Or perhaps you're looking for a partner who shares similar life goals and aspirations. Making these distinctions can pave the way for a relationship built on mutual understanding and harmony.

Lastly, keep your list flexible and open to surprises. While it's important to have standards and boundaries, remember that people are complex and multifaceted. Someone might not fit every detail on your list perfectly, but they could still be an amazing match in unexpected ways. Stay open-minded and willing to explore connections that might not initially meet all your criteria—you might just discover a connection that surpasses your expectations and brings joy to your life. Ultimately, making a list is about empowering yourself to recognize and pursue a relationship that enriches your life and aligns with your deepest desires.

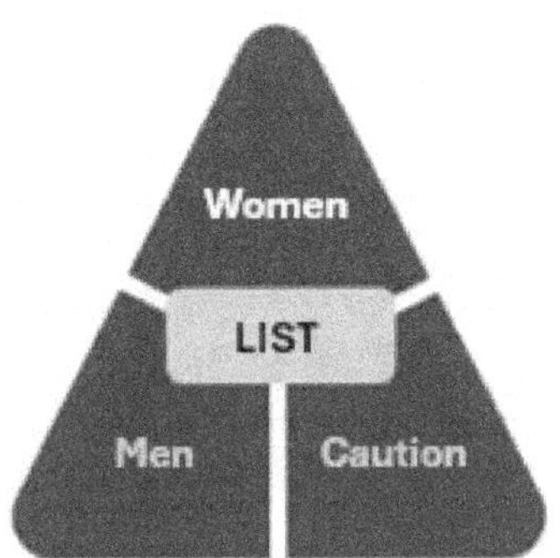
Women
LIST
Men
Caution

Women

Here are some qualities that many women often appreciate in men:

1. **Sense of Humor:** A good sense of humor can lighten any situation and create a connection based on laughter and fun.
2. **Confidence:** Confidence shows that you believe in yourself and can handle challenges with grace and composure.
3. **Kindness and Empathy:** Being caring and understanding demonstrates emotional intelligence and makes for a supportive partner.
4. **Respectfulness:** Treating others with respect, including waitstaff and strangers, shows consideration and integrity.
5. **Ambition and Drive:** Having goals and working towards them can be inspiring and show determination.
6. **Good Communication Skills:** Being able to listen actively and express thoughts clearly fosters understanding and connection.
7. **Shared Values:** Aligning important beliefs and values can create a strong foundation for a meaningful relationship.
8. **Emotional Maturity:** Handling emotions and conflicts calmly and responsibly reflects maturity and stability.
9. **Loyalty and Commitment:** Demonstrating loyalty to friends and family and being committed to the relationship shows dedication.
10. **Physical Attraction:** While personality is crucial, physical attraction and taking care of oneself can also be important factors.

Remember, everyone is unique, and preferences vary widely. Being authentic and true to yourself while embodying these qualities can help you connect with someone who appreciates you for who you are.

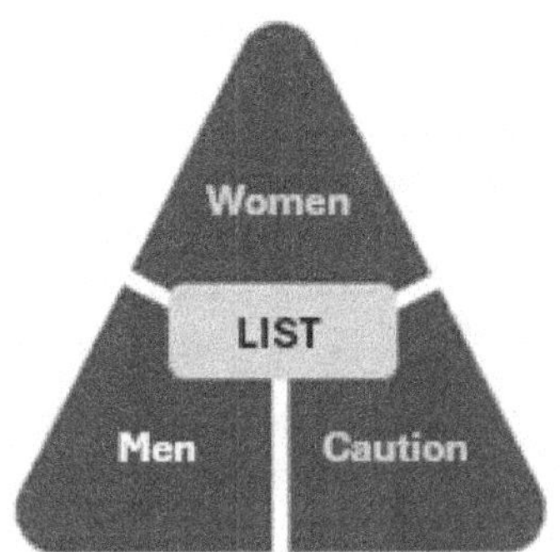
Women
LIST
Men
Caution

Men

Here's a list of qualities that many men often appreciate in women:

1. **Sense of Humor:** A woman who can share a laugh and enjoy playful banter is often seen as engaging and fun to be around.
2. **Kindness and Compassion:** Showing empathy and kindness towards others demonstrates a caring and nurturing personality.
3. **Confidence:** Confidence in oneself is attractive as it shows self-assurance and a positive self-image.
4. **Intelligence and Curiosity:** Intellectual curiosity and the ability to engage in meaningful conversations can be very appealing.
5. **Independence:** Having personal goals and interests outside of the relationship shows strength and self-sufficiency.
6. **Physical Attractiveness:** While personality is key, physical attraction and taking care of oneself can also be important factors.
7. **Shared Interests:** Sharing hobbies or activities can create bonds and opportunities for shared experiences.
8. **Trustworthiness:** Being reliable and trustworthy in actions and words builds a foundation of trust in the relationship.
9. **Supportiveness:** Being supportive of their partner's goals and dreams shows encouragement and belief in their abilities.
10. **Emotional Compatibility:** Understanding and managing emotions well can lead to better communication and a stronger connection.

Remember, these qualities can vary from person to person, and what's most important is finding someone who appreciates and values you for who you are. Being yourself and embracing these positive traits can help you build a meaningful and fulfilling relationship.

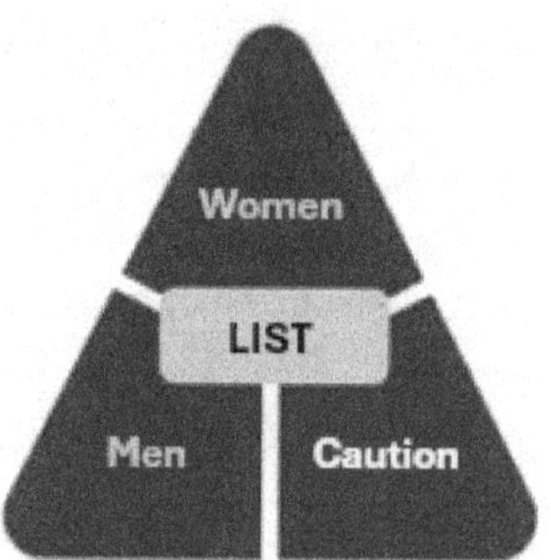

Women
LIST
Men
Caution

Caution

Here are some friendly reminders for both men and women to keep in mind while dating:

1. **Online Safety:** Be cautious about sharing personal information too quickly online. Take your time to get to know someone before revealing sensitive details.
2. **Setting Boundaries:** It's important to set and respect boundaries early on. Communicate openly about what you're comfortable with and listen to your date's boundaries as well.
3. **Moving Too Fast:** Take your time to build a connection. Rushing into intimacy or making big commitments too soon can sometimes cloud judgment.
4. **Red Flags:** Pay attention to behaviors that raise concerns, such as disrespect towards others, inconsistency, or overly controlling behavior. Trust your instincts and don't ignore warning signs.
5. **Emotional Honesty:** Be honest about your intentions and feelings. Leading someone on or playing games can hurt both parties in the long run.
6. **Physical Safety:** When meeting someone new, especially for the first time, choose public places and let a friend or family member know your plans. Safety first!
7. **Comparisons to Past Relationships:** Avoid constantly comparing your date to ex-partners. Each person is unique, and focusing on the present can lead to more genuine connections.
8. **Over idealization:** While it's natural to be excited about a new relationship, try to see your date realistically. Putting someone on a pedestal can lead to disappointment if they don't live up to unrealistic expectations.
9. **Communication Breakdowns:** Misunderstandings can

happen easily, especially via text or online messaging. If something feels off, clarify and communicate openly rather than making assumptions.

10. **Self-Care:** Dating should be enjoyable and fulfilling. Take breaks if you're feeling overwhelmed or stressed. Prioritize your own well-being and happiness throughout the process.

Remember, dating is an opportunity to explore connections and learn about yourself and others. Keeping these points in mind can help you navigate the dating scene with confidence and respect for yourself and others.

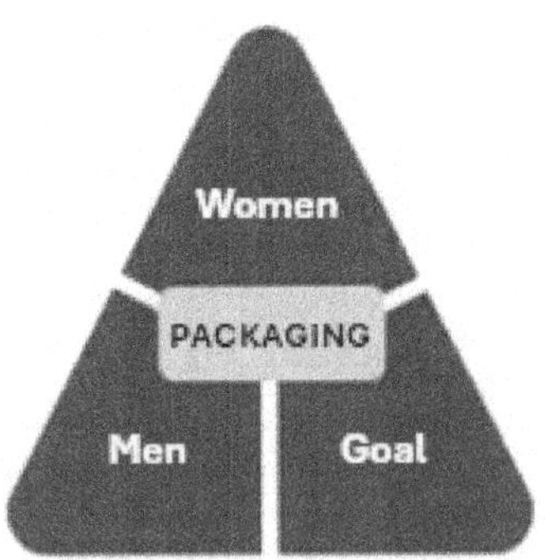
Women
PACKAGING
Men
Goal

PACKAGING

Packaging yourself for dating success is all about presenting your best self while staying true to who you are. Think of it as highlighting your strengths and unique qualities in a way that resonates with potential partners. This doesn't mean putting on a façade or pretending to be someone you're not. Instead, it's about showcasing your genuine personality, interests, and values in a positive light. Just like you might dress up for a job interview to make a good impression, presenting yourself well in dating can attract the kind of connections you're looking for.

First impressions matter, whether it's through your appearance, conversation skills, or how you express yourself online. Pay attention to how you present yourself in these areas, aiming to be approachable, confident, and genuine. This can involve anything from choosing flattering outfits that make you feel good to engaging in meaningful conversations that showcase your interests and passions. Remember, authenticity is key; being true to yourself will attract people who appreciate you for who you are.

Moreover, packaging yourself effectively involves clear communication about your intentions and what you're looking for in a relationship. This helps set expectations from the start and avoids misunderstandings down the road. Whether you're seeking a casual connection or a long-term commitment, being upfront about your goals shows respect for both you and your potential partners. It also fosters an environment of openness and honesty, which are crucial for building meaningful connections. By packaging yourself thoughtfully and authentically, you're not only enhancing your dating success but also creating opportunities for genuine connections based on mutual understanding and compatibility.

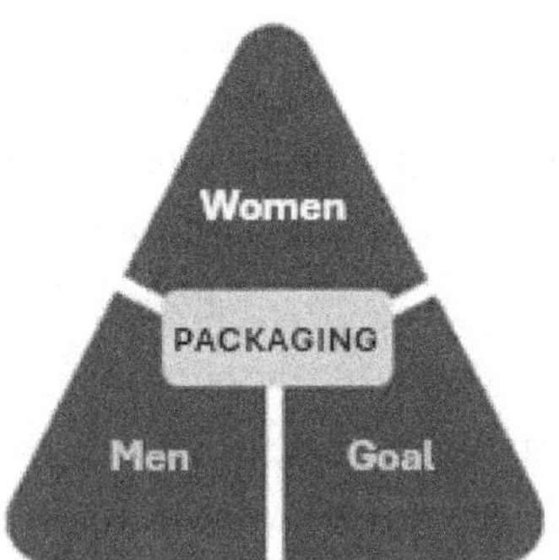
Women
PACKAGING
Men
Goal

Women

Packaging yourself effectively as a woman while dating involves embracing your unique qualities and presenting them confidently. Start by highlighting your strengths and interests—whether it's your sense of humor, intelligence, or passion for certain hobbies. These are aspects of your personality that make you special and can attract someone who appreciates you for who you are. When you feel good about yourself and what you bring to the table, it radiates positivity and confidence, which are attractive qualities in any relationship.

Physical appearance plays a role too, but it's not just about looks; it's about feeling comfortable and confident in your own skin. Choose outfits that make you feel empowered and express your personal style. When you're comfortable and confident in how you present yourself physically, it enhances your overall demeanor and makes a positive impression on others.

Communication is also key in packaging yourself effectively while dating. Express yourself clearly and honestly about your values, goals, and what you're looking for in a partner. This helps set expectations early on and ensures that you're both on the same page. Being open about your intentions shows maturity and respect for yourself and your potential dates. Remember, authenticity is attractive—embrace who you are, communicate openly, and let your genuine self shine through. When you package yourself in a way that reflects your true self and what you're looking for in a relationship, you're more likely to attract meaningful connections with someone who appreciates and values you for who you are.

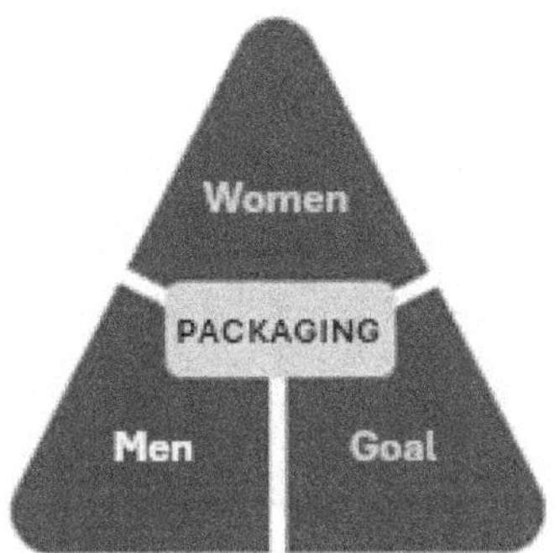

Women
PACKAGING
Men
Goal

Men

Packaging yourself effectively as a man while dating involves showcasing your best qualities while staying true to who you are. Start by emphasizing your strengths—whether it's your sense of humor, intelligence, ambition, or kindness. These are aspects of your personality that make you unique and can attract someone who appreciates you for who you are. Confidence is key here; when you believe in yourself and what you have to offer, it naturally draws others towards you.

Physical appearance and grooming also play a role in how you present yourself. While it's important to feel comfortable in your own skin, putting effort into your appearance shows that you care about how you present yourself to others. Choose clothes that make you feel confident and showcase your personal style. When you feel good about how you look, it boosts your self-esteem and makes a positive impression on potential partners.

Effective communication is another crucial aspect of packaging yourself while dating. Be open and honest about your intentions, interests, and what you're looking for in a relationship. This clarity helps establish trust and ensures that both parties are on the same page from the beginning. Listening actively to your date's interests and perspectives also shows respect and creates a strong foundation for meaningful connections. Remember, authenticity and sincerity are attractive qualities. When you package yourself in a way that reflects your true self and communicates what you're looking for in a relationship, you increase your chances of forming genuine connections with someone who values and appreciates you for who you are.

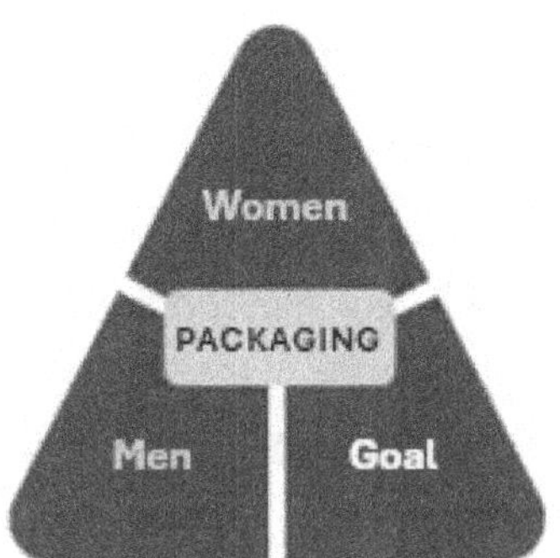
Women
PACKAGING
Men
Goal

Goal

Having a clear goal in mind while dating can be incredibly beneficial—it's like having a compass that guides your journey through the dating landscape. Whether you're looking for a casual relationship, exploring possibilities, or seeking a long-term commitment, defining your goal helps you navigate with intention and clarity. It's about knowing what you want and being upfront about your expectations, which can save time and prevent misunderstandings for both parties involved.

When you have a clear goal, it allows you to approach dating with confidence and purpose. You can focus your energy on meeting people who align with your relationship goals and values, increasing the likelihood of finding a compatible partner. This clarity also empowers you to make decisions that are in line with your desires, whether it's pursuing a deeper connection with someone special or respectfully moving on if the relationship doesn't meet your criteria.

However, it's important to remain flexible and open to unexpected connections and experiences along the way. Sometimes, the best relationships unfold organically when you least expect it. Having a clear goal doesn't mean rigidly sticking to a checklist; rather, it provides a framework for understanding your own needs and preferences while staying open to the possibilities that each new connection brings. Ultimately, dating is a journey of self-discovery and building meaningful connections, and having a clear goal can enhance this experience by guiding you towards relationships that fulfill your aspirations and bring joy into your life.

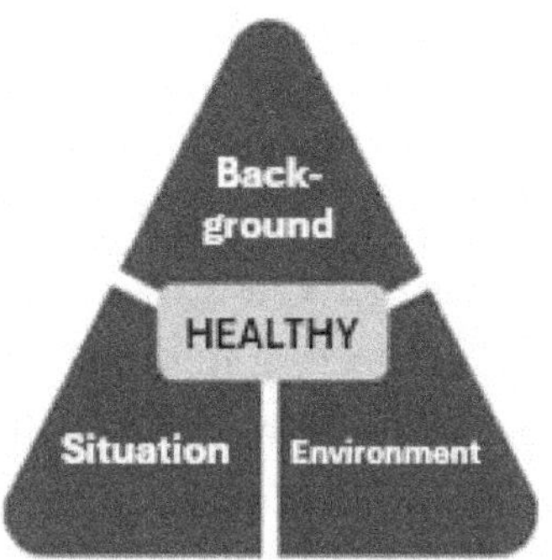

Back-
ground
HEALTHY
Situation
Environment

HEALTHY

The operative word in any relationship, personal or business, is HEALTHY.

It has been said that when you have two healthy people come together, the chances of a healthy relationship are very good. Conversely, when you have one unhealthy person or both unhealthy...this is a recipe for disaster in most cases.

Forging a healthy relationship with a mate is like nurturing a precious garden—it requires care, attention, and mutual respect to thrive. Healthy relationships are built on a foundation of trust, communication, and mutual support. Trust forms the bedrock of any strong relationship; it's about having faith in each other's words and actions and being reliable and dependable. When trust is present, it creates a safe space where both partners can be vulnerable and open without fear of judgment.

Effective communication is another cornerstone of a healthy relationship. It's not just about talking, but also listening actively and empathetically to your partner's thoughts and feelings. Clear and honest communication fosters understanding, resolves conflicts constructively, and strengthens emotional bonds. It's important to express your needs and concerns openly while being respectful of your partner's perspective, creating a dialogue that nurtures mutual growth and connection.

Moreover, supporting each other's growth and well-being is crucial in a healthy relationship. This means celebrating each other's successes, encouraging personal development, and being there through challenges and triumphs. Healthy relationships are partnerships where both individuals feel valued, appreciated, and understood. By prioritizing trust, communication, and mutual support, you cultivate a relationship that not only withstands the tests of time but also brings fulfillment and joy to both partners involved.

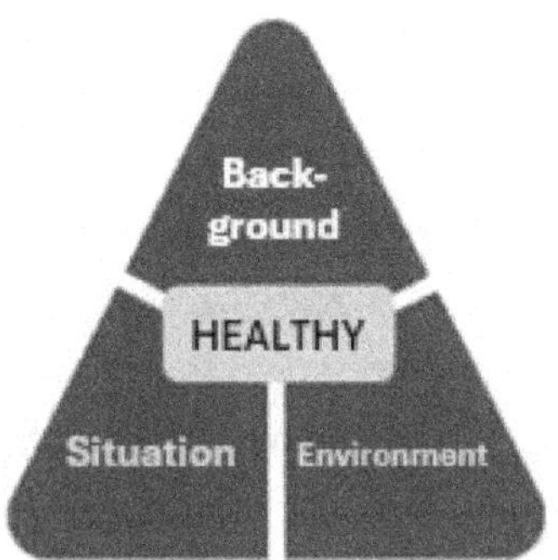
Back-
ground
HEALTHY
Situation
Environment

Background

Doing a background check on someone you've just met through dating can be a wise step in today's digital age, akin to ensuring your safety belt is securely fastened before embarking on a journey. While it might sound formal or overly cautious, it's about taking care of yourself and making informed decisions. Checking someone's background can provide valuable insights into their past and help verify the information they've shared with you.

Firstly, a background check can offer peace of mind by confirming basic details such as their identity, employment history, and education. It's a way to verify that the person you're getting to know is who they say they are. This transparency builds trust from the outset and lays a foundation of honesty in your budding relationship.

Secondly, conducting a background check can alert you to any red flags or inconsistencies that may warrant further discussion or consideration. While everyone has a past, knowing certain aspects—like legal records or previous relationships—can help you make informed decisions about your safety and compatibility. It's an opportunity to gather information that might not come up naturally in early conversations but could impact your future together.

Lastly, approaching a background check with sensitivity and respect is crucial. It's not about prying into someone's life but rather about ensuring compatibility and safeguarding your own well-being. Transparency is key; discussing your intention to conduct a background check openly and respectfully demonstrates your commitment to building a relationship based on trust and mutual respect. Ultimately, while it's important to approach dating with an open heart, it's equally important to approach it with a clear mind and a commitment to your own safety and happiness.

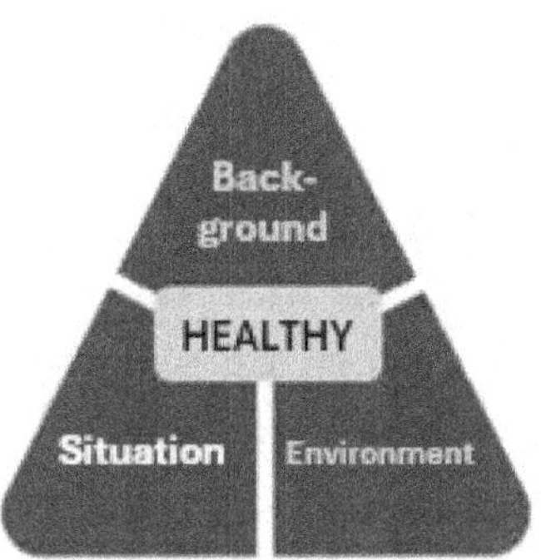

Back-
ground
HEALTHY
Situation
Environment

Situation

Analyzing someone's situation before dating them or deciding to date them is like taking a moment to read the map before starting a journey—it helps you understand where they're coming from and where they might be headed. This thoughtful approach can save both parties from potential misunderstandings and mismatches down the road. By analyzing someone's situation, you're essentially gathering information about their life circumstances, priorities, and readiness for a relationship.

Firstly, understanding someone's situation allows you to assess compatibility. Are they emotionally available and looking for the same type of relationship as you? Knowing where they stand in terms of their career, family commitments, and personal goals can give you valuable insights into whether your lifestyles and future aspirations align.

Secondly, analyzing someone's situation helps you gauge their readiness for a relationship. Are they in a stable place emotionally and financially? Are there any ongoing challenges or responsibilities that might impact their availability or ability to fully invest in a relationship? These considerations are important for building a relationship that has the potential to grow and thrive.

Lastly, taking the time to analyze someone's situation demonstrates respect and empathy. It shows that you care about understanding their life circumstances and are interested in forming a connection that is meaningful and supportive for both parties. Open communication plays a crucial role here; discussing each other's situations openly and honestly fosters understanding and strengthens the foundation of trust from the very beginning. Ultimately, analyzing someone's situation before dating is about making informed decisions that prioritize compatibility, readiness, and mutual respect, setting the stage for a relationship that has the potential to flourish.

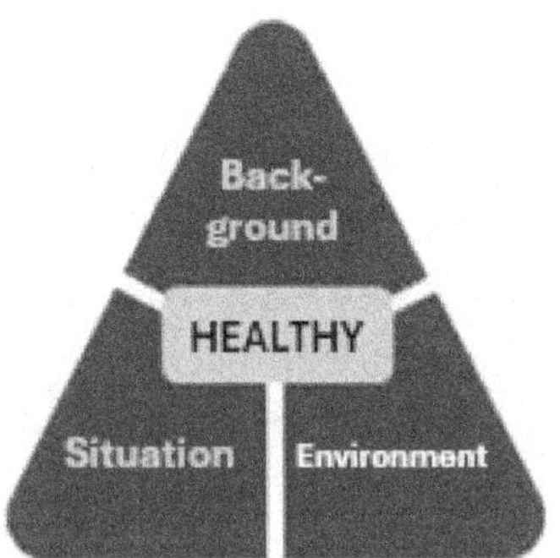

Back-
ground
HEALTHY
Situation
Environment

Environment

Analyzing someone's environment before dating them or deciding to pursue a relationship is akin to understanding the setting in which a story unfolds—it provides context and insight into their daily life, influences, and dynamics. This thoughtful approach allows you to gain a deeper understanding of their world beyond initial impressions, helping you make informed decisions about compatibility and future possibilities.

Firstly, analyzing someone's environment involves paying attention to their surroundings, such as their home, workplace, and social circle. These aspects can reveal a lot about their lifestyle, interests, and priorities. For example, their living space may reflect their organizational style and personal tastes, while their social circle can offer insights into their values and the kind of relationships they prioritize.

Secondly, understanding someone's environment allows you to assess how it might impact your potential relationship. Are they surrounded by supportive friends and family? Do they have a healthy work-life balance that allows room for personal growth and relationship building? These factors can influence their availability, emotional well-being, and ability to invest in a new relationship.

Lastly, analyzing someone's environment fosters empathy and connection. It shows that you're interested in understanding their world and appreciating the influences that shape who they are. This approach encourages open communication and mutual understanding, laying the groundwork for a relationship built on trust and compatibility. By taking the time to analyze someone's environment with curiosity and respect, you're better equipped to navigate the complexities of dating and build a meaningful connection that enhances both of your lives.

Women
LIST
Men
Caution
Women
PACKAGING
Men
Goal
DATING
Back-
ground
HEALTHY
Situation
Environment

SUMMARY

Dating indeed takes effort—it's like planting seeds in a garden and nurturing them to grow. It's not just about waiting for luck to strike but actively engaging in the process with intention and dedication. Putting effort into dating means taking initiative, putting yourself out there, and actively seeking opportunities to meet new people and build connections. This could involve joining social activities, trying out dating apps, or simply being open to meeting new people through friends and acquaintances.

Moreover, effort in dating means investing time and energy into getting to know someone genuinely. It's about asking thoughtful questions, actively listening, and showing genuine interest in their thoughts and feelings. Building a connection takes mutual effort and communication. It's not about expecting everything to fall into place effortlessly but rather understanding that building a meaningful relationship requires patience, understanding, and effort from both parties involved.

Lastly, while luck can sometimes play a role in meeting someone special, relying solely on luck can be passive. Taking an active role in your dating journey empowers you to make choices that align with your values and goals. It allows you to learn and grow from each interaction, whether it leads to a lasting connection or not. By putting in the effort and being proactive in your approach to dating, you increase your chances of finding a compatible partner who shares your interests and values. Remember, dating is a journey of self-discovery and connection-building, and by embracing the effort involved, you're setting the stage for meaningful relationships to flourish.

Invitation

There are no perfect people therefore there are no perfect relationships. Having said that, there are healthy and unhealthy relationships. The goal is to work toward and have healthy relationships in all areas of our lives. We do that by making a list and choosing to stick with it. My personal dating experience was a little different than most as I married my high school sweetheart (the only person I ever dated). Then after 25 years, I became single for the first time as an adult. I had no clue how to date or what the process was for dating, so mistakes were made along the way. My invitation to you is to benefit from the mistakes I made! Your life will go a lot smoother; I promise you.

My first mistake with dating is that I was on the rebound (but didn't realize it). That means I was desperately looking for someone to hurry and replace the person I had been with for a long time. Naturally, my approach was much too fast and needy. Then a professional therapist shared with me to take some time to heal before jumping into the dating game.

My second mistake was making a list so long that no one could possibly fit everything that I had listed. I think I had 17 things that must happen before I would be interested in someone. Fortunately, I came to my senses and reduced that list to three things that were preferred.

There were more mistakes made along the way, but I plowed through them and got better at the dating game. The one lesson I came away with from all this dating experience is that time is the great indicator. Here's what I mean: For the first 90 days, most of us are on our best behavior. Then after that...you'll start to see some things that you may or may not be comfortable with. After six months, then the real person starts to come out and their situations come to light. If all is well after that, then go ahead and make it a year before committing to anything. And here's why.

You will see all that you need to see in 12 months with holidays, birthdays, job situation, vacation, any sicknesses plus friends and family. Once that has transpired, then you should have a really good idea if doing something long-term makes sense. After all, what's the rush? Take your time to make it right. You can thank me later ;-)

When you're with someone who is sharing their struggles with you...just smile at him/her and give them one of these. He/she will ask "What is that?" Then simply reply "Life Works in Threes."

Other titles coming out:

- Weight Struggles?
- Abundance Struggles?
- Parenting Struggles?
- Life Struggles?
- Purpose Struggles?
- Happiness Struggles?
- Sales Struggles?
- Speaker Struggles?
- Time Struggles?
- Network Struggles?
- Marriage Struggles?
- Divorce Struggles?
- Money Struggles?
- Career Struggles?
- Romance Struggles?
- Caretaker Struggles?
- Forgiveness Struggles?
- Grieving Struggles?
- Success Struggles?
- Golf Struggles?
- Workplace Struggles?
- Stress Struggles?
- Shame/Guilt Struggles?
- Addiction Struggles?

Remember,

When you get right down to it,

Life is about making choices.

Every day, all day long, that's what we do.

- *We choose to get out of bed or not.*
- *We choose to clean up or not.*
- *We choose what to eat all day.*
- *We choose to exercise or not.*
- *We choose to go to work or not.*
- *We choose to do a good job or not.*
- *We choose to come home or not.*
- *We choose to watch TV or do something constructive.*
- *We choose to bed at a decent hour or not.*

And the next day...we start all over again.

What is the meaning of this? Get good at choosing.

Before you can get good at choosing though...you need to understand how life works in threes.

Creating a timeline for dating before getting serious can vary greatly depending on personal preferences and relationship dynamics. However, here's a general guideline that many people find useful:

1. Initial Attraction and First Dates (0-1 Month)

- **First Impressions:** Get to know each other through casual conversation and shared activities.
- **Multiple Dates:** Aim for a few dates to gauge chemistry and compatibility.
- **Communication:** Begin to establish regular communication but keep it light and fun.

2. Building Connection (1-3 Months)

- **Deeper Conversations:** Start discussing more personal topics, values, and future goals.
- **Consistency:** Regular communication and spending time together.
- **Introduce to Friends/Family:** If the connection feels strong, start introducing each other to close friends or family.

3. Evaluating Compatibility (3-6 Months)

- **Discuss Relationship Goals:** Talk about what each of you is looking for in a relationship and whether your goals align.
- **Handle Conflicts:** Observe how you handle both disagreements and conflicts.
- **Quality Time:** Spend more quality time together and engage in activities that reveal more about each other's habits and preferences.

4. Defining the Relationship (6-12 Months)

- **Have the "DTR" Conversation:** Define the relationship (DTR) and discuss exclusivity and commitment.
- **Meet Each Other's Inner Circles:** If you haven't already, meet each other's close friends and family.
- **Discuss Future Plans:** Start talking about long-term goals and plans to see if they align.

5. Committing to a Serious Relationship (12+ Months)

- **Evaluate Long-Term Compatibility:** Reflect on the relationship's progress and whether it meets your long-term expectations.
- **Discuss Major Milestones:** Talk about significant future milestones, such as moving in together, marriage, or children, if relevant.
- **Commitment:** If both partners feel ready, make a formal commitment to a more serious and long-term relationship.

Additional Tips:

- **Personal Pace:** Adjust the timeline according to personal comfort and relationship dynamics.
- **Communication:** Keep open lines of communication throughout the process to ensure both partners are on the same page.
- **Flexibility:** Be flexible and understanding, as relationships can evolve differently for each couple.

This timeline is just a general framework and should be adapted to fit individual situations and relationship dynamics.

Quotes about Dating

"The best relationships start off as friendships first." — Unknown

"Dating is not about finding someone to live with. It's about finding someone you can't imagine living without." — Unknown

"In the end, it's not going to matter how many dates you went on, how many times you were hurt, or how many times you were in love. What will matter is that you were true to yourself and followed your heart." — Unknown

"The right person will make you feel like a better version of yourself." — Unknown

"When you're dating, you don't need to know where you're going. You just need to know that you're going together." — Unknown

"Dating is a lot like a deck of cards. In the beginning, all you need is two hearts and a diamond. By the end, you're looking for a club and a spade." — Unknown

"Sometimes the person you're looking for is right in front of you. You just need to look with your heart instead of your eyes." — Unknown

"Dating is the art of getting to know someone well enough to know if you want to see them naked." — Unknown

"It's not about finding someone who is perfect. It's about finding someone who is perfect for you." — Unknown

"The best relationships are the ones you didn't see coming." — Unknown

My Personal Dating Experience

After marrying my high school sweetheart and divorcing some 20 years later, I was new to the dating game at age 40ish. Needless to say, I had no clue how to go about dating. It was kind of like getting back on a bicycle but a little tougher than that.

I dated for about 10 years and met some wonderful ladies along the way. The one mistake I made (because I just didn't know better) is that I got involved with a lady from out of state. She had moved to my city recently and joined the singles group of the church I was attending.

The mistake I made was…I didn't know anyone that knew her. So therefore, I had no background information or history on this person. Nine months later, I found out some things that were dealbreakers for me. From then on, I made sure that I knew someone that knew the person I was dating to save heart ache and disappointment down the road.

Just saying.

When someone is struggling with a particular area or two, chances are they are "out of balance" with how life works. How does life work? Life works in threes.

If you're interested in personal topics like life, health, money or business topics like sales, time management and public speaking...TRYUNE WORKS! can shed some light on creating success in those areas.

The definition of TRIUNE is a group of three things; united. Being three in one, such as - humans are mental, physical and spiritual beings. The word TRYUNE is a play of the word TRIUNE, encouraging all to try this concept and help eliminate struggling unnecessarily.

LifeWorksInThrees.com

* 9 7 9 8 2 2 4 9 0 4 5 9 4 *